For the Teacher

This reproducible study guide to use in conjunction with a specific novel consists of lessons for guided reading. Written in chapter-by-chapter format, the guide contains a synopsis, pre-reading activities, vocabulary and comprehension exercises, as well as extension activities to be used as follow-up to the novel.

In a homogeneous classroom, whole class instruction with one title is appropriate. In a heterogeneous classroom, reading groups should be formed: each group works on a different novel on its reading level. Depending upon the length of time devoted to reading in the classroom, each novel, with its guide and accompanying lessons, may be completed in three to six weeks.

Begin using NOVEL-TIES for reading development by distributing the novel and a folder to each child. Distribute duplicated pages of the study guide for students to place in their folders. After examining the cover and glancing through the book, students can participate in several pre-reading activities. Vocabulary questions should be considered prior to reading a chapter; all other work should be done after the chapter has been read. Comprehension questions can be answered orally or in writing. The classroom teacher should determine the amount of work to be assigned, always keeping in mind that readers must be nurtured and that the ultimate goal is encouraging students' love of reading.

The benefits of using NOVEL-TIES are numerous. Students read good literature in the original, rather than in abridged or edited form. The good reading habits, formed by practice in focusing on interpretive comprehension and literary techniques, will be transferred to the books students read independently. Passive readers become active, avid readers.

Novel-Ties® are printed on recycled paper.

SYNOPSIS

When Mr. Murry disappeared, people gossiped that he had abandoned his family. Only his young son Charles Wallace seemed to have some insight into his father's whereabouts. Mrs. Murry was too absorbed in her laboratory research and the ten-year-old twins, Sandy and Dennys, were too busy with sports and their own friends to worry. But Meg Murry was wounded by the evil gossip and feared that her father was in mortal danger.

An adventure into the world of the fifth dimension, or the act of tessering, begins as the three supernatural Mrs. W's—Mrs. Who, Mrs. Which, and Mrs. Whatsit—take Meg, Charles Wallace, and their friend Cal on a mission to rescue Mr. Murry. At first, they only know that father's scientific research into the principle of the "Tesseract" has gotten him into this predicament.

Their journey takes them to the beautiful planet Uriel, past the ominous "Black Thing," to the dreadful planet Camazotz where Mr. Murry is held captive. Unable to accompany them to this planet, the Mrs. W's leave the children to their own resources, hoping they can resist the hypnotic power of the Man with the Red Eyes. Despite his powers of clairvoyance, Charles Wallace succumbs and becomes an unfeeling, robot-like creature as are all the others on this planet.

It is Meg, wearing Mrs. Who's special spectacles, who penetrates the transparent column that imprisons Mr. Murry. Once outside the column, Meg, Cal, and Mr. Murry resist the controlling, hateful power of IT and tesser off the planet Camazotz.

After a short respite on the planet Ischel, Meg is chosen to return to Camazotz to retrieve Charles Wallace. Using the strength of her love, she succeeds in releasing her brother from the evil control of IT and returning them all to the planet Earth.

PRE-READING ACTIVITIES

1. Preview the book by reading the title and the author's name and by looking at the picture on the cover. What do you think the book will be about? Do you think it will be a fantasy or realistic fiction? Have you read any other books by the same author?

2. What do you think would cause a person your age to feel inferior to others? Which of these qualities could someone change and which ones would have to be accepted.

3. Think about a time when nothing went right for you no matter how hard you tried. What was the occasion? Who was involved? Whose fault was it? Did one bad situation lead to another?

4. Brainstorm with your classmates to make a list of all the ways people communicate with one another. Record all responses on the chalkboard. After you have exhausted all of the conventional responses, discuss para-normal means of communication, such as ESP.

5. Imagine another place in the universe where life could exist among people with a higher degree of intelligence than our own. Describe what this place might be like. How might one creature of higher intelligence subjugate everyone else?

6. What do you think would happen if each of the following wishes came true? Include good and bad results in your answer.
    - Everyone had a college education.
    - No one was poor or unemployed.
    - Children weren't required to go to school.
    - Everyone always told the truth.
    - Everyone had the same strength, skills, and mental ability.

7. Have you read any books, seen any films, or watched any TV programs in which people traveled away from the planet Earth? How were these people depicted? How were the worlds they visited described in books, films, or on television? Do you think there is any truth to the fiction you encountered? Did any of the books, films, or TV programs convey a lesson or a moral?

8. In what category of books, films, or television programs are you likely to find clearly defined characters who are either good or evil? What characteristics of appearance separate these characters? How do their activities separate them? As you read *A Wrinkle in Time*, notice whether the characters fall into categories of good or evil, or whether there are those who more realistically have elements of both.

9. Use the Story Map on the following page to jot down important events while you read *A Wrinkle in Time*. Also, keep track of characters and places. This will help you as you read about the children's complicated journey. The first chapter has been done for you.

STORY MAP

Title	Events
Chapter 1	• All members of the Murry family are introduced on the night of the hurricane: Mrs. Murry, twins, Meg, Charles Wallace. • Father has been absent for a long time—reason unclear. • Mrs. Whatsit arrives. She is a strange lady, who only CW knows, who makes a mysterious remark about a "Tesseract."
Chapter 2	
Chapter 3	
Chapter 4	
Chapter 5	
Chapter 6	

Story Map (cont.)

Title	Events
Chapter 7	
Chapter 8	
Chapter 9	
Chapter 10	
Chapter 11	
Chapter 12	

CHAPTER 1 – MRS. WHATSIT

Vocabulary: Draw a line from each word on the left to its meaning on the right. Then use the numbered words to fill in the blanks in the sentences below.

1. uncanny
2. vulnerable
3. relinquish
4. sullen
5. serenity

a. calmness; well-being
b. weird; mysterious
c. give up
d. glum; ill-humored
e. easily hurt or wounded

. . . .

1. Sitting at the shore of a calm lake gives me a feeling of _____.

2. My friend had a(n) _____ ability to know what I was going to say ahead of time.

3. The little boy became _____ when none of his friends would play with him.

4. A home at the beach is _____ to storm damage.

5. If you will _____ your claim to this piece of land the bank will pay you twenty thousand dollars.

Etymology: Although English is a Germanic language, it has been enriched by additions from many sources, including Greek and Latin. Here are some words from Chapter One that have a Latin origin:

Word	Meaning	Origin
diction	manner of expressing ideas in words	from Latin *dictio*–a saying, speech
liniment	soothing liquid which is rubbed on the skin to relieve pain or stiffness	from Latin *linimentum*–ointment, from *linire*–to smear
prodigious	wonderful; marvelous	from Latin *prodigiosus*–strange, marvelous, from *prodigium*–portent, omen
subdued	conquered; overcame by superior force	from Latin *subdere*–to subjugate, bring under

Chapter 1 (cont.)

Read to find what is special about the Wallace family.

Questions:

1. What is most unusual about Mrs. Whatsit?

2. How does Meg feel about herself? Why does she have these feelings?

3. What is unusual about Charles Wallace?

4. How does Mrs. Whatsit upset Mrs. Murry?

Questions for Discussion:

1. Why do you think Mrs. Murry is upset by Mrs. Whatsit?

2. What mysteries are left unsolved at the end of Chapter One? Why do you think the author has left these questions unanswered?

Literary Technique: Light and Dark Imagery

Madeleine L'Engle has used images of light and dark throughout the book to suggest good and evil respectively. As you continue to read the book indicate, on a chart such as the one below, those people, places, and events that point up this comparison.

Chapter	Good / Light	Evil / Dark

Writing Activity:

Use your imagination and what you have learned so far in the book to write about one of the mysteries at the end of Chapter One. As you continue to read, see whether your story matches the one you find later on in the book.

Chapter 1 (cont.)

Literary Elements: Fill in the chart below to record what you have learned in Chapter One. Then write a prediction telling what you think will happen in the story.

Setting *Where* and *when* the story takes place.	At what place does the story begin? At what time of day does the story begin? What is the atmosphere at that time?
Characters *Who* appears in the story.	Who are the members of the Murry family, and what do you know about each one?
Plot *What* occurs in the story.	What has happened?
What do you think will happen in this story? 	

CHAPTER 2 – MRS. WHO

Vocabulary: Synonyms are words with similar meanings.Draw a line from each word in column A to its synonym in column B. Then use the words in column A to fill in the blanks in the sentences below.

A		B	
1.	belligerent	a.	wisely
2.	sagely	b.	impulse
3.	dilapidated	c.	absorb
4.	compulsion	d.	hostile
5.	antagonists	e.	adversaries
6.	assimilate	f.	ruined

. . . .

1. The _____ faced each other from opposite sides of the ring before the fight began.

2. The judge nodded _____ when the witness described a logical pattern of events.

3. If you cannot control your _____ to eat rich foods, you will ruin your health.

4. He studied hard and was able to _____ every fact in the chapter.

5. If we buy this _____ house, we will have to make many repairs.

6. Your _____ attitude is keeping you from making new friends.

Etymology:

The word "sinister" comes from the Latin word *sinister*, which means "left" or "on the left side." It was believed in ancient times that the left side was unlucky. Gradually the meaning of sinister changed to evil. Compare the meaning of the word "sinister" with the meaning of the word "dexterous," which comes from the Latin *dexter*, which means "on the right side." Are these words opposites in English as they are in Latin?

> Read to find out why Meg is unhappy.

Questions:

1. How does Mrs. Murry respond when Meg asks her to define a "tesseract"?

2. Why does Meg get into trouble at school? How does the principal make matters worse?

Chapter 2 (cont.)

3. Why does Charles Wallace hide his special talent?

4. How are Calvin and Charles alike?

5. Why does Charles want to visit the three women? Why does Meg go along?

6. Who is Mrs. Who? What is unusual about her way of speaking?

7. What does Charles mean when he tells Cal, "Meg has it tough. She's not really one thing or another"?

Questions for Discussion:

1. Do you think exceptional children need to hide their special qualities from others their own age?

2. What do you think Calvin means when he says, "I've never seen your house, and I have the funniest feeling that for the first time in my life I'm going home"?

Language Activity: Proverbial Play

A proverb is a short, popular saying that expresses a well-understood truth. Mrs. Who uses proverbs to communicate meaning. What do you think each of these proverbs means:

1. Don't count your chickens before they hatch.

   _____

2. A rolling stone gathers no moss.

   _____

3. A stitch in time saves nine.

   _____

4. A bird in the hand is worth two in the bush.

   _____

5. Don't put all your eggs in one basket.

   _____

6. The early bird catches the worm.

   _____

Writing Activity:

Write about a time when you or someone you know got into trouble at school because there was a problem at home. Describe the incident and tell how the problem at home affected life at school.

CHAPTER 3 – MRS. WHICH

Vocabulary: Draw a line from each word on the left to its meaning on the right. Then use the numbered words to fill in the blanks in the sentences below.

1.	somber	a.	wise
2.	tangible	b.	feeling angry at something unfair
3.	essence	c.	the most important part of something
4.	judicious	d.	that which can be touched or understood
5.	indignant	e.	gloomy; sad

. . . .

1. If you do not listen carefully, you will miss the _____ of my lesson.

2. The little girl became _____ because she had to go to bed earlier than all of her friends.

3. It is traditional to wear the _____ colors of black or gray when attending a funeral.

4. You will be able to make a(n) _____ decision after you hear both sides of the argument.

5. A jury is supposed to assume a person innocent unless there is _____ proof of guilt.

> Read to find out how Charles surprises Meg and Cal.

Questions:

1. What does the photograph of Mr. Murry reveal about his past? What else do we learn about him in this chapter?

2. What is Meg's special talent? Why does she have difficulty in school despite this talent?

3. What startling announcement does Charles make to Meg and Cal?

4. What does Cal mean when he says that the children in school like him for all the wrong reasons?

5. What clue reveals that the Mrs. W's are extraordinary women?

Questions for Discussion:

1. Do you know anyone like Meg who has trouble in school despite being smart?

2. What do you think Mrs. Murry could mean when she says that Charles is "new"?

Chapter 3 (cont.)

Literary Device: Foreshadowing

Foreshadowing refers to the clues an author provides to suggest what is going to occur later on in the novel. How did the author foreshadow Charles's startling announcement, "We're going"?

_____

_____

_____

Writing Activities:

1. Both Cal and Meg feel that they are misunderstood by others. Tell about one way in which you think others misjudge you. Do you want to change this? Does it make you unhappy?

2. Write about the one character in the book so far who is the most like you. Provide specific examples of instances in your own life and in the book that point up these similarities.

CHAPTER 4 – THE BLACK THING

Vocabulary: Draw a line from each word on the left to its meaning on the right. Then use the numbered words to fill in the blanks in the sentences below.

1. metamorphose   a. great happiness

2. fragments   b. change the form of something

3. infinite   c. put out; cause to end

4. extinguish   d. parts; pieces broken off

5. bliss   e. without end; space without boundaries

. . . .

1. When the plate dropped to the tile floor, _____ of china fell everywhere.

2. Cinderella knew that her carriage would _____ into a pumpkin at midnight.

3. Be sure to _____ the ashes in the campfire before you go to sleep.

4. There seem to be a(n) _____ number of stars in the sky.

5. An expression of _____ came to the young girl's face when she learned that she would soon see her long-lost father.

> Read to find out what is wonderful and what is frightening as the children begin their travels.

Questions:

1. Where do the children land on their first stop? How would you describe this place? What was terrifying about their passage?

2. What happens to Mrs. Whatsit when she removes her clothes? How do the children feel about her new appearance?

3. Why does Mrs. Whatsit give each child a flowerlet bell?

4. What scares Meg as they travel away from Uriel?

5. What does Meg believe the Black Thing could be?

Chapter 4 (cont.)

Questions for Discussion:

1. What do you think Mrs. Who means when she utters the proverb, "The more a man talks, the less he knows"? Have you ever known the truth of this proverb?

2. What conclusions can be drawn about Charles Wallace since he is the only one of the children who can understand unspoken communication?

Art Connection:

1. Reread the beginning of Chapter Four and use water color or pastel chalk to illustrate Uriel, the planet that was used for a rest stop.

2. Illustrate how you imagine the appearance of the "Black Thing."

Writing Activity:

Pretend you are either Meg, Charles Wallace, or Cal and you are taking an incredible journey. Write a diary entry describing your thoughts and feelings.

CHAPTER 5 – THE TESSERACT

Vocabulary: Antonyms are words with opposite meanings. Draw a line from each word in column A to its antonym in column B. Then use the words in column A to fill in the blanks in the sentences below.

<u>A</u>   <u>B</u>

1. perturbed   a. contentment
2. plaintively   b. peaceful
3. anxiety   c. happily
4. reproved   d. excitedly
5. serenely   e. applauded

. . . .

1. The child was _____ for leaving skates on the staircase.

2. The pilot's _____ increased as the storm raged and the gas supply dwindled.

3. The teacher was _____ when no one in class handed in the assignment on time.

4. She called out to her old friend _____ as the train pulled away from the station, taking her away forever.

5. Although everyone expected him to become hysterical, he accepted his football team's defeat _____.

Word Study:

The word "medium" has several meanings. Some of these meanings are:

- middle state or condition
- intervening substance, like air, through which a force acts
- means or form of communication
- person through whom the spirits of the dead are alleged to be able to contact the living

As you read this chapter, find at least two ways in which the word "medium" is used. How does the author consciously play on several meanings of the word?

> Read to find out what happens to the children on the second stop of their journey.

Chapter 5 (cont.)

Questions:

1. What is the purpose of the children's journey?

2. According to the book, what is the first dimension? the second? the third? the fourth? the fifth? Which of these terms relate to known geometry and which are fictional?

3. According to the book, what does it mean "to tesser"?

4. What technical mistake does Mrs. Which make as she continues the journey? What happens to the children as a result?

5. Describe the second stop on the journey.

6. What is the Black Thing? How have people throughout the ages been fighting the Black Thing?

7. Why do the three Mrs. W's dislike speech, preferring to communicate in another way?

Questions for Discussion:

1. Have you ever feared something like the Black Thing? What form has it taken in your life?

2. Why do you think Mrs. Which takes the children to visit the medium on the way to their destination?

Literary Devices:

I. *Cliffhanger*—A cliffhanger is a device borrowed from silent, serialized films in which an episode ends at a moment of heightened tension. In a book it is usually placed at the end of a chapter. What is the cliffhanger at the end of Chapter Five?

II. *Foreshadowing*—How were the following events in Chapter Five foreshadowed:

- tessering
- finding a happy medium
- fighting the dark thing

III. *Analogy*—An analogy is a point by point comparison between two dissimilar objects for the purpose of clarifying the lesser known object What analogy does the author use to explain the act of tessering?

Writing Activity:

Write about the Black Thing as you imagine it to be. How might it appear and what, specifically, does it represent?

CHAPTER 6 – THE HAPPY MEDIUM

Vocabulary: An analogy is an equation in which the first pair of words has the same relationship as the second pair of words. For example: QUESTION is to ANSWER as ASCEND is to DESCEND. Both pairs of words are opposites. Use the words in the word box to fill in the blanks in the analogies below.

WORD BOX		
apprehension	falter	resilience
arrogance	malignant	talisman

1. EXTENDED is to REDUCED as BENIGN is to _____.

2. FRAGILITY is to CRYSTAL as _____ is to CONCRETE.

3. HUMILITY is to _____ as WISDOM is to IGNORANCE.

4. _____ is to GOOD FORTUNE as BACTERIA is to ILLNESS.

5. DETERMINATION is to FORGE AHEAD as WORRY is to _____.

6. _____ is to FEAR as PEACE is to CONTENTMENT.

> Read to find out why Camazotz is a frightening place for Charles.

Questions:

1. What is Mrs. Whatsit's origin?

2. Why haven't the children been fed since they left earth?

3. What is Camazotz, and why have the children gone there? What is the most unsettling characteristic about life on Camazotz?

4. What warning does Mrs. Which give the children as she leaves them alone on Camazotz?

5. How does Charles feel as the children prepare to enter the Central Intelligence Building?

6. Why is Charles frightened of the people on Camazotz?

Chapter 6 (cont.)

Questions for Discussion:

1. Why do you think Mrs. Who quoted from Shakespeare's play *The Tempest* as a hint for the children?

2. Camazotz is different from any place on Earth. In what ways is it significantly different from your town?

3. In what ways do you think Mrs. Whatsit's parting gifts to each of the children may prove to be important?

Literary Device: Allusion

An allusion is an indirect reference to something relatively well-known within a culture. For example, a New York newspaper's slogan of "Truth, Justice, and the Comics" is an allusion to *Superman's "Truth, Justice, and the American Way."* Use a dictionary to help you determine how Camazotz may be an allusion to "Camelot."

_____

_____

_____

Writing Activities:

1. Mrs. Whatsit told Meg to "Stay angry. . . . You will need all your anger now." Write about a time when you used anger to help you accomplish something that you would not ordinarily have done.

2. The Medium complains, "If I didn't get fond I could be happy all the time." Write about a situation in which your fondness for someone or something inadvertently caused you unhappiness.

3. Write about one of your own personality traits that would be most valuable in a dangerous place like Camazotz.

CHAPTER 7 – THE MAN WITH RED EYES

Vocabulary: Use the context to determine the meaning of the underlined word in each of the following sentences. Then draw a line from each word on the left to its meaning on the right.

1. We worried that no one would come to our rescue in a <u>remote</u> snow-bound ski house.

2. If you are <u>tenacious</u> enough, you will achieve your goal.

3. Even though we were extremely thirsty, we would not dare drink the <u>bilious</u> tasting water.

4. The diver's <u>bravado</u> as he climbed to the top if the high-diving board masked the fear he felt inside.

5. The new student felt some fear as she crossed the <u>threshold</u> of her classroom on her first day of school.

. . . .

1.	remote	a.	holding fast
2.	tenacious	b.	any place or point of entering
3.	bilious	c.	swaggering display of courage
4.	bravado	d.	distant; far
5.	threshold	e.	extremely distasteful

> Read to find out what happens when Charles meets the man with the red eyes.

Questions:

1. Who is the man with red eyes? What is he trying to do to the children?

2. Why does Charles hit the man?

3. How does the man communicate with the children without using language?

4. How is Charles changed after submitting to the man's power?

Chapter 7 (cont.)

5. Why does Charles eventually submit to the man with red eyes? Why is it better for Charles rather than for Cal or Meg to submit to him?

6. What do you think Meg means when she shrieks at Calvin, "That isn't Charles! Charles is gone"?

Questions for Discussion:

1. Why do you think that Charles is the only child who finds that the food tastes terrible?

2. The man with the red eyes offers to "assume all the pain, all the responsibility, all the burdens of thought and decision" for the children. Discuss the reasons for and against living in a society where individuals have relinquished all decision-making to the government.

3. How is education on Camazotz different from your own? Are there any aspects of schooling there that should be adopted in your school? Are there any aspects that are similar to your own school?

Figures of Speech:

A figure of speech is an expression that does not mean what it says. For example, "It's raining cats and dogs," means that it is raining very hard, not that animals are literally falling from the sky. In *A Wrinkle in Time*, the author plays with figures of speech so that they have the same literal and figurative meaning. How does this apply to Meg when she "knocks him [Charles Wallace] to his senses?

_____

_____

_____

Writing Activity:

A utopia has come to mean an ideal or perfect place. It derives from the sixteenth-century book *Utopia*, written by Sir Thomas More, in which he described an island that enjoyed a perfect political system and thus, a perfect society. Write about a place that would be your utopia: describe its educational system, its government, and its general living conditions. Then compare your utopia to that of Camazotz.

CHAPTER 8 – THE TRANSPARENT COLUMN

Vocabulary: Draw a line from each word on the left to its meaning on the right. Then use the numbered words to fill in the blanks in the sentences below.

1. bland
2. submit
3. ominous
4. deviate
5. misconception
6. annihilate

a. threatening; foreboding
b. incorrect idea
c. agreeable; soothing
d. destroy completely
e. turn from
f. yield in surrender

. . . .

1. Will the children _____ to the strange forces they encounter?

2. The children feared that the power of IT could _____ them.

3. The _____ bank of dark clouds loomed above them.

4. Don't _____ from your regular route or you will get lost.

5. Charles Wallace tried to convince Meg that her fears about Camazotz were based on a(n) _____ about the planet.

6. _____ food seems tasty to the inhabitants of Camazotz.

> Read to find out how Charles Wallace changes and yet remains the same.

Questions:

1. In what ways has Charles Wallace changed since he came to Camazotz? In what ways is he the same?

2. Who directs the children to Mr. Murry?

3. What happens to people on Camazotz who dare to be different? What happens to those who fall ill?

4. Where is Mr. Murry?

5. Why does Charles Wallace say, "Mrs. Whatsit, Mrs. Who, and Mrs. Which have confused us. They're the ones who are really our enemies"?

6. Although Meg has suffered for being "different" on earth, why does she now defend the right to be different?

Chapter 8 (cont.)

Questions for Discussion:

1. What happens to children who dare to be different? Might they suffer?

2. Can adults live happy lives if they dare to be different?

3. In what ways is your life controlled by adult or governmental authority?

Writing Activity:

Write about whether you agree or disagree with Charles when he says, "On Camazotz we are all happy because we are all alike. Differences create problems." Tell whether or not you think differences cause problems. Provide examples to support your opinion.

CHAPTER 9 – IT

Vocabulary: Draw a line from each word on the left to its meaning on the right. Then use the numbered words to fill in the blanks in the sentences below.

1. inexorable
2. transparent
3. endurance
4. omnipotent

a. almighty; all powerful
b. unyielding; not able to be changed
c. clear; possible to see through
d. patience

. . . .

1. The _____ ruler would not allow freedom of speech or freedom of the press.

2. In order to survive brutal conditions, prisoners adopted an attitude of _____.

3. It is pointless to argue with a(n) _____ decision.

4. The water in the lake was so _____ that brightly colored fish could be seen swimming at the bottom.

> Read to learn how Meg is able to reach her father.

Questions:

1. How has Mr. Murry been imprisoned on Camazotz? What have been the conditions of his imprisonment?

2. What does Cal hope to accomplish by staring at Charles?

3. What purpose do Mrs. Who's spectacles serve Meg inside the column?

4. What is IT? How does Meg try to fight the hypnotizing rhythm of IT?

5. How is Meg rescued from IT's control?

6. Why is Meg disappointed in her father after they are reunited?

7. What does Meg mean when she says, "like and equal are two different things"?

Questions for Discussion:

1. Why do you think it was Meg, and not Charles or Cal, who rescued Mr. Murry?

2. How do you think the children and Mr. Murry will escape from Camazotz?

Chapter 9 (cont.)

Profound Confusion:

The pronoun "it" refers to a thing. Reread the sentences below in which Charles mentions "IT" five times. On the lines below, tell what "IT" refers to in each case.

IT[1] wants you and IT[2] will get you. Don't forget that I, too, am part of IT,[3] now. You know I wouldn't have done IT[4] if IT[5] weren't the right thing to do.

1. _____

2. _____

3. _____

4. _____

5. _____

Writing Activity:

Write about objects or incidents that illustrate Meg's belief that "like" and "equal" are two different things.

CHAPTER 10 – ABSOLUTE ZERO

Vocabulary: Draw a line from each word on the left to its meaning on the right. Then use the numbered words to fill in the blanks in the sentences below.

1. imperceptible
2. emanate
3. revulsion
4. hostile
5. fallible

a. strong feeling of dislike
b. able to make mistakes; imperfect
c. not friendly; antagonistic
d. very slight; not detected by the senses
e. come forth; originate

. . . .

1. Her poor manners at the table filled me with _____.

2. By the end of the day her perfume was almost _____.

3. His _____ attitude toward everyone he knew caused him to lose many friends.

4. There are erasers on pencils because its users are _____.

5. A sense of fear seemed to _____ from the civilians as they heard the fighter planes approach overhead.

> Read to find out if the children and Mr. Murry all leave Camazotz.

Questions:

1. How did Mr. Murry get to Camazotz?

2. What is Meg's physical reaction when she is tessered away from Camazotz? Why does she feel this way?

3. Why doesn't Mr. Murry know how long he has been away from Earth?

4. Why do Mr. Murry and Cal agree to leave Charles Wallace behind in Camazotz?

5. Why is Meg angry with her father?

6. Why are Meg and Cal afraid of the beasts at first? How does their experience illustrate the old saying, "Do not judge a book by its cover"?

Question for Discussion:

Do you think Mr. Murry acted intelligently or in a cowardly fashion when he left Charles on Camazotz?

Chapter 10 (cont.)

Readers Theatre:

Present Chapter Ten as Readers Theatre to the entire class. One student can play the role of Mr. Murry, another play the role of Meg, and a third play the role of Cal by reading the words in the quotations as dialogue. A fourth student can serve as narrator.

Writing Activity:

Meg has always admired her father to such a degree that she suffers terrible disappointment when she finds that he cannot save Charles. Write about a time when you have been disappointed by someone you admired. Tell whether this experience taught you any important lessons.

CHAPTER 11 – AUNT BEAST

Vocabulary: Choose the best word from the Word Box to complete each of the analogies below.

WORD BOX		
eternal	opaque	trepidation
grave	tentacle	

1. DARK is to LIGHT as TEMPORAL is to _____.

2. PERSON is to ARM as OCTOPUS is to _____.

3. SERIOUS is to _____ as CANDID is to FRANK.

4. SMILE is to SCOWL as COURAGE is to _____.

5. GLASS is to TRANSPARENT as WOOD is to _____.

> Read to learn about the kindness of the beasts.

Questions:

1. How does Meg recover from her tessering experience?

2. Why don't the beasts understand the concepts of "light," "dark," or "opaque"?

3. Why is Meg angry and unhappy even though she is no longer in pain from her tessering experience?

4. Why does Aunt Beast find it difficult to understand and answer Meg's questions?

Questions for Discussion:

1. What do you think Calvin means when he tells the beast that they are from a shadowed, not a dark, planet?

2. What do you think Aunt Beast means when she says, "We look not at the things which you would call seen, but at the things which are not seen. For the things which are seen are temporal. But the things which are not seen are eternal"?

Writing Activity:

Write about examples from your own experience that illustrate Aunt Beast's statement above.

CHAPTER 12 – THE FOOLISH AND THE WEAK

Vocabulary: Draw a line from each word in column A to its synonym in column B. Then use the words in column A to fill in the blanks in the sentences below.

A		B	
1.	formidable	a.	detest
2.	reiterate	b.	repeat
3.	loathe	c.	feared
4.	eerie	d.	weird

. . . .

1. I _____ the taste of whole wheat bread even though it is healthier than white bread.

2. Because I knew he would be a(n) _____ tennis opponent, I practiced for hours before the match.

3. The _____ setting was appropriate for the mystery film.

4. Listen carefully the first time because I will not _____ my instructions.

> Read to find out what happened to time while the children were away.

Questions:

1. Why does Meg, rather than Cal or Mr. Murry, have to be the one to rescue Charles Wallace?

2. What gift does Mrs. Whatsit give Meg as protection before she begins her second trip to Camazotz?

3. What does Meg accomplish on her own on this second trip?

4. How does Meg succeed in rescuing Charles from the power of IT?

5. How do we know that the children have only been gone for less than a day in Earth time?

Chapter 12 (cont.)

Questions for Discussion:

1. How do you think Meg has been changed by her recent experiences?

2. Although *A Wrinkle in Time* is fantasy, what parts of the story or the experiences of the characters are realistic?

3. Do you think life in general is easier for people like the twins or for people like Meg and Charles Wallace?

Writing Activities:

1. Write about the ways that life on Earth may be like a sonnet. Give examples to explain your meaning.

2. Write about the quality that Meg has, but IT has not. Explain why this is an important quality.

CLOZE ACTIVITY

The following passage has been taken from Chapter Four of the novel. Read it through entirely. Then fill in each blank with a word that makes sense. Afterward, you may compare your language with that of the author.

The trees were lashed into a violent frenzy. Meg screamed and clutched at Calvin, _____[1] Mrs. Which's authoritative voice called out, "_____,[2] chilldd!"

Did a shadow fall across _____[3] moon or did the moon simply _____[4] out, extinguished as abruptly and completely _____[5] a candle? There was still the _____[6] of leaves, a terrified, terrifying rushing. _____[7] light was gone. Darkness was complete. _____[8] the wind was gone, and all _____.[9] Meg felt that Calvin was being _____[10] from her. When she reached for _____[11] her fingers touched nothing.

She screamed _____,[12] "Charles!" and whether it was to _____[13] him or for him to help _____,[14] she did not know. The word _____[15] flung back down her throat and _____[16] choked on it.

She was completely _____.[17]

She had lost the protection of _____[18] hand. Charles was nowhere, either to _____[19] or to turn to. She was _____[20] in a fragment of nothingness. No _____,[21] no sound, no feeling. Where was _____[22] body? She tried to move in _____[23] panic, but there was nothing to _____.[24] Just as light and sound had _____,[25] she was gone, _____.[26] The corporeal Meg simply was not.

POST-READING ACTIVITIES

1. Use a chart, such as the one below, to compare Meg at the beginning and at the end of the novel.   **Meg**

Beginning of Novel	End of Novel

2. **Cooperative Learning Activity:** Work with a small group of your classmates to compile a list of ten people who brought light, hope, and goodness to our world. Then rank these people on a scale of one to ten. Finally, compare your list with the lists of others in your class.

3. Return to the Story Map that you began on page three of this study guide. Complete your notes for each chapter. If you were to locate the turning point of the novel, or the climax, in what chapter would you say it occurred? What single event might be considered the turning point?

4. Some people view this book as a tale of good *versus* evil. If this is true, how are good and evil represented in the story? What qualities are considered good and what qualities are considered evil? How is evil conquered in the novel?

5. Do you think our planet is seriously threatened by a "Black Thing"? What are some of the manifestations of the Black Thing in our world today? Do you think people will overcome these dangers or eventually submit to the Black Thing?

6. The inhabitants of Camazotz were all alike. Discuss the concept of "conformity." Do you see conformity as having an effect on your life? What are some of the negative effects of conformity? What are some of the positive effects? Write a poem or essay on the evils or the benefits of conformity.

7. Discuss the idea of extra-sensory perception (ESP). Charles Wallace always seemed to know about an event before it occurred. Could this have been ESP? Have you ever felt that you or someone near to you was experiencing ESP?

8. Name some other science fiction stories you have read. What science fiction movies or television programs have you seen? Describe the science fiction elements in them to the class. What makes good science fiction?

9. Explain the meaning of some of the following statements and tell how each one relates to the novel *A Wrinkle in Time*:
    *   The road to Hell is paved with good intentions.
    *   Faith is the sister of justice.
    *   Nothing deters a good man from doing what is honorable.
    *   The only way to cope with deadly seriousness is to treat it lightly.
    *   How small is the Earth to him who looks from heaven.
    *   The light shineth in darkness but the darkness comprehendth it not.
    *   There is nothing to fear but fear itself.

Post-Reading Activities (cont.)

10. Consult newspapers or magazines to find examples of people who have been punished for daring to differ from their governments. Indicate the nature of the disagreement and assess the justification of the punishment.

11. Here is a list of adjectives that describe people. Use a dictionary to learn the meaning of those words you do not know. List those adjectives that are appropriate for each of the characters shown below. You may use a word more than once and add additional adjectives to describe each character.

awkward	grim	intuitive	sage
clairvoyant	impatient	loyal	sensitive
compassionate	impetuous	ominous	stubborn
domineering	insecure	perceptive	arrogant
gentle	intelligent	responsible	tender

Charles Wallace	The Happy Medium	IT
Meg	**The Black Thing**	**Aunt Beast**
Mrs. Whatsit	**Mrs. Who**	**Mrs. Which**

SUGGESTIONS FOR FURTHER READING

* Babbitt, Natalie. *Tuck Everlasting*. Farrar, Straus & Giroux.

Baum, Lyman Frank. *The Wonderful Wizard of Oz*. Penguin.

* Bradbury, Ray. *Fahrenheit 451*. Ballantine.

* Carroll, Lewis. *Alice's Adventures in Wonderland*. Scholastic.

* Christopher, John. *The White Mountains*. Simon & Schuster.

* Cooper, Susan. *The Dark is Rising*. Simon & Schuster.

Huxley, Aldous. *Brave New World*. HarperCollins.

* Lewis, C. S. *The Lion, the Witch and the Wardrobe*. HarperCollins.

* Lowry, Lois. *The Giver*. Random House.

Mazer, Norma. *Saturday, the Twelfth of October*. Random House.

Merriam, Eve. *Ab to Zuff*. Simon & Schuster.

* Nelson, O. T. *The Girl Who Owned A City*. Random House.

* O'Brien, Robert. *Z for Zachariah*. Random House.

* Orwell, George. *1984*. New American Library.

Pearce, Phillipa. *Tom's Midnight Garden*. Random House.

* Sleator, William. *Interstellar Pig*. Random House.

* Tolkien, J. R. R. *The Hobbit*. Ballantine.

Some Other Books by Madeleine L'Engle

And Both Were Young. Random House.

The Arm of the Starfish. Random House.

Camilla. Random House.

Dragons in the Waters. Random House.

Meet the Austins. Random House.

The Moon by Night. Random House.

A Ring of Endless Light. Random House.

A Swiftly Tilting Planet. Random House.

A Wind in the Door. Random House.

The Young Unicorns. Random House.

* NOVEL-TIES Study Guides are available for these titles.

ANSWER KEY

Chapter 1
Vocabulary: 1. b 2. e 3. c 4. d 5. a; 1. serenity 2. uncanny 3. sullen 4. vulnerable 5. relinquish
Questions: 1. Mrs. Whatsit wears layers of unusual clothes, yet moves with great agility. She also seems to be clairvoyant. 2. Meg has poor self-esteem because she thinks she is ugly and dumb. 3. Charles is exceptionally bright, yet most outsiders think he is abnormally stupid. He has a remarkable vocabulary and is able to read minds. 4. Mrs. Whatsit tells Mrs. Murry that there really is a phenomenon known as a "tesseract."

Chapter 2
Vocabulary: 1. d 2. a 3. f 4. b 5. e 6. c; 1. antagonists 2. sagely 3. compulsion 4. assimilate 5. dilapidated 6. belligerent
Questions: 1. Mrs. Murry is upset at the mention of the word "tesseract" and postpones explaining it to Meg. 2. Meg, worried about her family situation, cannot pay attention to schoolwork and then is rude when she is reprimanded. The principal makes matters worse by suggesting that Mr. Murry is gone for good. 3. Charles has the unusual talent of reading people's minds. He pretends to be stupid so that people will hate him less. 4. Both Calvin and Charles are very intelligent and are clairvoyant. 5. Charles wants to warn the women not to display the sheets they had stolen and to beware of youthful pranksters. Meg goes along because she wants to learn more about Mrs. Whatsit and her two friends. 6. Mrs. Who appears to be another old woman who lives with Mrs. Whatsit. It is unusual that she speaks many languages and constantly uses proverbs. 7. Charles means that Meg is neither "normal" enough to be one of the gang at school, nor as brilliant or clairvoyant as her little brother.

Chapter 3
Vocabulary: 1. e 2. d 3. c 4. a 5. b; 1. essence 2. indignant 3. somber 4. judicious 5. tangible
Questions: 1. The photograph reveals that Mr. Murry has worked at Cape Canaveral. He has been involved in top-secret government work, and now no one seems to know where he is. 2. Meg's talent is mathematics. This causes her trouble in school because her father taught her so many shortcuts that she has trouble doing math the way it is taught in school. 3. Charles makes the startling announcement to Meg and Cal that they are setting out to find Father. 4. Cal means that his classmates don't appreciate his brains, but rather they admire him for his less important athletic prowess. 5. The three women have the extraordinary ability to materialize out of thin air.

Chapter 4
Vocabulary: 1. b 2. d 3. e 4. c 5. a; 1. fragments 2. metamorphose 3. extinguish 4. infinite 5. bliss
Questions: 1. On their first stop, the children land on the planet Uriel, an ideally beautiful place with flowers everywhere. It is inhabited by beautiful creatures. They had to pass through a dark, empty space to get there. The total absence of light and sound during their passage was terrifying. 2. When Mrs. Whatsit removes her clothes, she metamorphoses into a marble-like figure with the body of a horse, a human torso, and rainbow wings. The children are enraptured with her new form. 3. Mrs. Whatsit gives each of the children a flowerlet bell to help them breathe at a high altitude where the air is thin. 4. As they travel away from Uriel, Meg is frightened by the dark shape out in the atmosphere. 5. Meg thinks it is the Black Thing that might be threatening her father.

Chapter 5
Vocabulary: 1. b 2. c 3. a 4. e 5. d; 1. reproved 2. anxiety 3. perturbed 4. plaintively 5. serenely
Questions: 1. The children begin a journey because they want to rescue Mr. Murry. 2. The first dimension is a line; the second is a flat shape; the third is a shape with depth, such as a cube; the fourth is the square of a shape, such as a cube, or time; and the fifth is the square of the fourth dimension, or a tesseract. The first, second, and third dimension are true geometric terms; the fourth and fifth dimensions are fictional. 3. To tesser is to travel in the fifth dimension, going through space without being hampered by the speed of light. 4. Mrs. Which takes the children to a two-dimensional planet by mistake. As a result, the children become flat. 5. The second stop is a planet that is so hazy that it is impossible to discern shapes. 6. The Black Thing is universal evil. Artists, writers, religious leaders, and other people of genius have been using their talents to combat the effects of evil. 7. The three Mrs. W's prefer their unspoken communication because it is more profound than speech.

Chapter 6
Vocabulary: 1. malignant 2. resilience 3. arrogance 4. talisman 5. falter 6. apprehension
Questions: 1. Mrs. Whatsit began life as a star who then lost her life as a martyr fighting the forces of evil. 2. The Mrs. W's do not need food and therefore have forgotten to feed the children. 3. Camazotz

is the planet where Mr. Murry will be found. It is unsettling to find that all of the people on the planet behave like robots. 4. Mrs. Which warns the children to stay together on the planet Camazotz. 5. As the children prepare to enter the Central Intelligence Building, Charles is worried because he cannot read what these people are thinking. 6. Charles is frightened because this is the first time he has ever encountered a mind he could not penetrate.

Chapter 7
Vocabulary: 1. d 2. a 3. e 4. c 5. b
Questions: 1. The man with red eyes seems to be the person in charge at the CENTRAL Central Intelligence Building. He is trying to hypnotize the children. 2. Charles hits the man with red eyes to find out if he is real. 3. The man communicates through thought instead of language. 4. After Charles submits to the man with red eyes, his voice becomes flattened out, and he does not seem to have emotions. 5. Charles thinks if he submits to the man and finds out what he is, he will be able to continue on to find his father. Charles thinks he will be able to release himself from the man's power once he learns about his father, but he fears the other children would not be able to do so. 6. Meg means that Charles has become part of the population controlled by IT. He appears to be the same, but his thoughts are no longer his own.

Chapter 8
Vocabulary: 1. c 2. f 3. a 4. e 5. b 6. d; 1. submit 2. annihilate 3. ominous 4. deviate 5. misconception 6. bland
Questions: 1. Since he came to Camazotz, Charles has become totally dispassionate and is mouthing the sentiments of the man with the red eyes. His outward appearance is unchanged. 2. Charles takes Meg and Calvin to Mr. Murry. 3. On Camazotz, people who deviate are punished. People who become ill are killed. 4. Mr. Murry is imprisoned inside a transparent column. 5. Charles is uttering the words of some powerful being on Camazotz. These would not be his sentiments if he were no longer under its control. 6. Meg now thinks it would much worse if everyone were the same, as on Camazotz.

Chapter 9
Vocabulary: 1. b 2. c 3. d 4. a; 1. omnipotent 2. endurance 3. inexorable 4. transparent
Questions: 1. Mr. Murry has been imprisoned on Camazotz inside a transparent column. He has been unable to see anything within or outside the column. 2. By staring at Charles Wallace, Cal hopes to pull him out of IT's control. 3. The spectacles allow Meg to penetrate the column in order to reach her father. 4. IT is a disembodied brain. Meg tries to fight IT's control by reciting the Declaration of Independence. 5. Meg is rescued from IT's control by intoning the table of square roots, and then by her father's act of tessering. 6. Meg is disappointed that her father does not comprehend Charles's condition. 7. The word "like" suggests sameness in all things physical and emotional. The word "equal" means being entitled to the same rights and privileges.

Chapter 10
Vocabulary: 1. d 2. e 3. a 4. c 5. b; 1. revulsion 2. imperceptible 3. hostile 4. fallible 5. emanate
Questions: 1. Mr. Murry had tessered as part of an experiment in the work that he did. Since he was inexperienced, he came to Camazotz by mistake. 2. When Meg tessers away from Camazotz, she suffers because she becomes frozen. 3. Mr. Murry does not know how long he has been away from Earth because time on Camazotz is not linear as it is on Earth. Therefore, he has lost track of time. 4. Mr. Murry and Cal leave Charles Wallace behind because they fear that if they do not leave quickly, both Cal and Meg will come under IT's power. 5. Meg is angry that her father left Charles Wallace behind. 6. At first, the beasts scare Meg and Cal because they are strange looking. It turns out that the beasts are very comforting.

Chapter 11
Vocabulary: 1. eternal 2. tentacle 3. grave 4. trepidation 5. opaque
Questions: 1. The beasts nurse Meg back to health after her tessering experience. 2. The beasts do not understand the concepts of "light," "dark," or "opaque" because they do not have the power of sight. 3. Meg is angry that Charles Wallace has been left behind. Her anger is also the product of the Black Thing that affected her when they last tessered. 4. The beasts cannot answer Meg's familiar with the language.

Chapter 12
Vocabulary: 1. c 2. b 3. a 4. d; 1. loathe 2. formidable 3. eerie 4. reiterate
Questions: 1. Meg must be the one to rescue Charles because she knows him best of all. 2. Mrs. Whatsit gives Meg the gift of that which she has that IT was not. 3. Meg rescues Charles on her second trip. 4. Meg uses her power of love to rescue Charles. 5. It is clear that less than a day in Earth time has passed when Dennys tells Meg it is bedtime and does not seem to know that she has been gone.